RUBEN GUTHRIE

CURRENCY PRESS
SYDNEY

Brendan Cowell

First published in 2009
by Currency Press Pty Ltd,
PO Box 2287, Strawberry Hills, NSW, 2012, Australia
enquiries@currency.com.au
www.currency.com.au
in association with
Company B Belvoir, Sydney.
Copyright © Brendan Cowell, 2009
This edition published in 2011
Reprinted 2012

NATIONAL LIBRARY OF AUSTRALIA CIP DATA

Author:	Cowell, Brendan 1976–.
Title:	Ruben Guthrie / Brendan Cowell.
ISBN:	9780868199238 (pbk.)
Dewey Number:	A822.4

Typeset by Dean Nottle for Currency Press.
Printed by SOS print+media, Alexandria, NSW.
Cover design by Emma Vine.

Contents

Ruben Guthrie was first produced by murri fulla films in association with B Sharp at Belvoir St Downstairs Theatre, Sydney, on 17 April 2008, with the following cast:

RUBEN GUTHRIE	Toby Schmitz
ZOYA	Samantha Reed
RAY	Christopher Stollery
PETER	Lex Marinos
VIRGINIA	Megan Drury
MUM	Tracy Mann
DAMIAN	Torquil Neilson

Director, Wayne Blair
Designer, Jacob Nash
Composer, Steve Francis
Lighting designer, Luiz Pampolha

CHARACTERS

RUBEN GUTHRIE, late 20s, handsome
ZOYA, 19 or 20, and thin
RAY, 45ish
PETER, late 50s, early 60s
VIRGINIA, late 20s, or even mid-late 30s
MUM, mid-late 50s
DAMIAN, late 20s, early 30s, and fit

AUTHOR'S NOTE

A '/' (or stroke) in the text indicates an interruption or overlap in the dialogue. Two slashes indicate where the second set of interruptions take place, and so on.

ACT ONE

1.1: A HALL

RUBEN *sits in a circle. His arm in a sling.*

RUBEN: Hello my name is Ruben Guthrie and I am…
    Here!
    In this lovely church hall, sitting in the circle—having a 'share'.
    I um, as you can see—from my face and arm, I ahhh… had a bit
if an incident. Accident.

      RUBEN *sings a line about accidents from 'You Can Call Me Al'.*

Paul Simon peaked with Graceland, he peaked. And then…
    Where were we? Group—yes my arm! Right we ahhh… had
the Federation of Advertising Awards on Saturday night, at which I
picked up the Gong for best ad and best ad campaign fourth year in
a row just quietly—and so maybe I imbibed a little on the wing of
my continuing success and decided to surprise everyone at the after
party by jumping off the roof of the very tall hotel.

    The ironic thing is I created the entire ad campaign: *How will you
feel tomorrow?*
    I um, I'm Creative Director of 'Subliminal'.
    Which is basically an Advertising Agency, but we also Brand
for companies/client, plus supply content and concept platforms for
online and interactive media—our stuff is pretty raw, like say we
do an ad for street wear we'll use real street kids not actors—shit
like that. For me it's an ARTFORM—like lately I've been thinking
Iraq you know, all those soldiers moving through civilian towns in
their tanks, rolling over huts securing premises 'n' shit—and I think
bam! Whack a Coke can in that scene; do you know what I mean?
And come on—I mean let's face it, if you were a soldier in Iraq,
and you'd just had a hard as fuck day controlling the chaos in that
searing dry fifty-degree Iraqi heat, wouldn't you be stinging for a
cold can?

Hot soldier rolls out of the situation, wipes the dust and shrapnel out of his hair… spots a machine, frosted over and fully stacked with rows of icy-cold black *love.*

I rest my case baby. Did someone say 'Truth in Advertising'?

And it *appals* me the way other agencies produce such manufactured, contrived like replicating, representations of, not, symbolically not representing… how life is—do you know what I mean?! Anyway. So my arm.

I look down over the guttering of the hotel roof; there must be a thousand Advertising types around the pool drinking and talking in black tie. I'm thinking this will go down in history as like, one of the coolest things ever to happen in the game—and you know, this kind of action is up to me, I am the designated renegade—so be my lease.

I took a hit from a little bag of Magic I had in my shirt pocket, knocked off the half bottle of Absolut Mandarin I snatched off Hot Waitress and crouched like Carl Lewis.

'Nothing can hurt you nothing can touch you. You're Ruben Guthrie.'

I'm running. And the edge comes quick and I'm out there!

I highly recommend it by the way; combination of 'caine, vodka, and *flight*—out with the eagles man, flapping my heavy wings and soaring I can fly—I'm flying—I can fly.

And I fucking judged it perfectly, landing smack bang in the middle of what I thought was a standard adult pool but soon discovered was actually a children's wading bath.

'Crack' was the noise that stopped the party. 'Lucky not to die' was the term they used in the hospital.

Didn't phase me—it's just a break it's all part of being a renegade you take the good with the bad and fuck… that's where people like me live, out on the edge man… and I try to explain that to *certain people,* but Mum and Zoya my fiancée here thought it was symbolic or something and that I should come to this place and admit…

Admit…

That I don't know the difference between a pool and a children's wading bath?

You guys must drink a lot of tea.

Is it compulsory to wear Kmart tracksuits or is it a coincidence that all of you are… wearing umm…

So look, I really appreciate you guys listening to me and everything and you all seem like a great bunch, I'd love to use you guys in something one day if I can find the right… *the right…*

But, ahh, yeah—I mean, after hearing your stories, like your tale Janelle about hiding in the roof of the bottle shop every night, and you Jeremy, oh and you Ken… KEN!!!! About drinking Jim Beam for breakfast then driving a forklift through your ex-wife's front window. I mean you guys—you guys need to lay off the sauce for shiz. I wouldn't be offering you guys a brandy chocolate if you were over my house.

Not even!

So yeah my name is Ruben Guthrie and I am in Advertising.

1.2: A KITCHEN

RUBEN *pops the cork from a champagne bottle. Pours two glasses.*

RUBEN: Champagne Zoya?!

Zoy'?! Champagne, I got Krug here—your favourite fizz!

ZOYA *enters with a wheelie-suitcase. She gathers bags and things throughout the scene, leaving and re-entering constantly.*

ZOYA: I have to go now.

RUBEN: Right now?

ZOYA: Yep.

RUBEN: Ok.

How long is the shoot for?

ZOYA: Um. The *shoot* is for three days.

RUBEN: Cool, you'll be home in three days then!

ZOYA: The shoot is in Munich Ruben, I told you but you were drunk so /again you ask.

RUBEN: /Munich Munich Munich yes!

ZOYA: I am going to the shoot then I am going home.

I am going now.

To go home.

RUBEN: Home?

I'm confused   you are home.

ZOYA: Home no to Prague.

Home to my mother's home.

My real home.

RUBEN: To visit—on your way through?

ZOYA: To stay. *Stay.*

RUBEN: You're fucking… you're going to…

> Holy shit… back up the truck—you're what!?

ZOYA: Going home to live with my mother yes…

RUBEN: Going home to live with your mother yes /and do what?

ZOYA: /Yes.

> I intend to study //and

RUBEN: //Study?? HA!

ZOYA: Just what I expect, this arrogant this…

RUBEN: You have no qualifications Zoya! I mean, ha! There certainly ain't
a huge swimsuit scene happening in downtown Prague is there?!

ZOYA: No Ruben there isn't.

> You got me with that one.

RUBEN: Zoya, oh come onnnnnn!

ZOYA: Goodbye red face.

RUBEN: Who's a red face? I got a tan face—I tan.

ZOYA: Not so *HQ Magazine* as when I met you.

> /Beer belly.

RUBEN: /You're fucking with me.

> Ha! Is this—ha!
>
> Is this all because of 'the pool incident'?

ZOYA: No, I like what the pool incident has done!

RUBEN: I don't see why you're making such a rash de/cision to leave
and—

> *She turns on him now.*

ZOYA: /All we do is box each other, in this two-bedroom ring—*every*
night!

> Me in the quiet corner—you in the drunken one.

RUBEN: I'm in meetings//now Zoya? *Meetings!*

ZOYA: //ONE meeting. You go to ONE meeting. Which your mother and
I *dragged* you to!

> And in that *one* meeting you went to humiliating us in front of
everyone in the church hall room and now you are drinking this ///
champagne and…

> RUBEN *holds up his glass.*

RUBEN: ///I'm celebrating my first meeting!

Car horn beeps.

ZOYA: Goodbye.

RUBEN: We're *engaged* Zoya.

That means you stick by each other, through sickness and in health.

ZOYA: No no. You do that when you're *married!*

RUBEN: Zoya.

You can't seriously be doing this to your life.

Please tell me that the last two years…

ZOYA: Three.

RUBEN: Three years have been worth something to you?

Supporting you through your whole depression eating disorder thing!

ZOYA: Oh. /My. God.

RUBEN: /Sorry, I shouldn't have, I didn't mean to…

ZOYA: Are you *comparing*…

RUBEN: I was there for you remember—is *all* I'm saying about—

ZOYA: What I go through is not a luxury!

Getting fucked up is a luxury.

A dumb stupid *childish* luxury and…

You see this is me, I do this to myself I over-eat.

Because I like to keep bad thoughts of me eat bingeing pain.

And then I see me with you, and I think this is the same thing as the over-eating.

You and the food you keep me here, in this black low place where I can hate myself and…

RUBEN: Ok, you've clearly been reading *Cleo* again.

ZOYA: Oh fuck off I do not read *Cleo* I read *books* Ruben *books*—when was the last time you read a book? You just read updates on your…

RUBEN: Ok, go.

ZOYA: What?

RUBEN: Good luck with your life.

ZOYA: Don't reverse psychologize this!

RUBEN: Do you know what you are breaking here?

ZOYA: Ruben, I warned you!

RUBEN: If you go now that is it, you lose it all.

We are no more!

Nothing. Dead. Over.

ZOYA: I just. I can't.

Literally, I don't know where you are or who you are with.

RUBEN: No more cuddles…

ZOYA: And the marks on your neck.

RUBEN: No more Ruben bringing home special cakes for after dinner.

ZOYA: And your breath!

RUBEN: Muffins, pain au chocolat, Danish tart.

ZOYA: Not anymore.

RUBEN: Chocolate mousse, chocolate truffles, Lindt.

RUBEN *touches her.*

We are so good together Zoya, remember.

She's the cheese and…

ZOYA: He's the macaroni.

RUBEN: Can you put your Donna Karan tote bag down and I'll tell you something?

You are so beautiful.

ZOYA: Fuck beautiful!

Fuck you and your beautiful advertisements and fuck me and my beautiful face.

I would cut into my face to show how I feel about this *beautiful* shit!

RUBEN: Zoya, sit down and have a glass of Krug.

I'll run you a bath and put your Dido albums on!

ZOYA: I am alone Ruben, like the photo shoots I do, page after pages of this young girl alone on a beach, those expressions I do, on those grey beaches, those *forlorn* looks and *demure* looks all *lost* and *confused* and *frightened*, they are me now, I have become those looks!

RUBEN: You look beautiful on the cover of German *Vogue.*

ZOYA: You think I look beautiful?

I think I look dead!

ZOYA *rolls her luggage out.*

RUBEN: Zoya, don't go—don't do this.

Zoya, don't leave me now.

Don't leave me on my own!

RUBEN *left alone.*

CUNT! YOU FUCKING CUNT YOU FUCKING CUNT YOU FUCKING TRY AND SURVIVE WITHOUT ME BITCH YOU'RE FUCKED—MODELS—HA! MODELS

HAVE A SHELF LIFE OF FUCKING TEN MINUTES YOU'RE FUCKEN GONE YOU
ARE YOU'RE GOING TO DIE IN THE FUCKING SNOW CHEWING YOUR OWN
HIPS YOU FUCKING WHORE YOU FUCKING TITLESS FUCKING—YOU CAN'T
SURVIVE WITHOUT RUBEN GUTHRIE—YOU'RE NOTHING WITHOUT HIM!
AAAAHHHHHHHHHH!

    RUBEN *swigs champagne. It fizzes and foams.*

1.3: A HALL

RUBEN: I mean, ok, I'm clearly not—
    I mean I'm not what you guys are.
    With the whole *title* and everything. So don't—look at me like—
    But I will admit to *favouring* a drink.
    It's un-Australian not to!
    And Advertising culture man the booze the pills the 'caine are
conducive, no… what's the word… *fundamental* to the way we
construct ideas, we have to tap into the mindset of the people, the
status quo, the unconscious… *conscience* of the consumer.

    RUBEN *drinks a litre of water in one go.*

'Blackouts'.
    Ok.
    A while ago I um.
    I don't know, I guess this is an example of it!
    Friday night end of the week Client drinks at Cargo Bar—y'know.
    Zoya was going to meet me at Tetsuya's at seven for the Deg—it
was her nineteenth birthday.
    What?
    I thought I'll hit Client drinks at five, nail two or three Peronis with
the Google guys then jump a cab to dinner, picking up some flowers
and a card on the way.
    Boom Guth!
    But it's summer in the city and I smash ten Peronis in a flash then
one of the G-guys scores some rack off a text message and it's fresh
from the good rock and it lands in the middle of my face with a thud
and a zing and a 'let's go baby' and we're flying first class one-way.
    Suddenly some post-folk band holding a warehouse party in
Darlington, IVY pool bar some slut in a blue bra   kick on   this
film actor's penthouse suite   I'm fingering this peacock-headed art

dealer in a spa bath full of Moët then bang! I'm on a motorbike arms wrapped round this hilarious lesbian gangster who takes me to her fibro shack way out west and we bump a mountain of ICE and drink a crate of bourbon surrounded by her thirty-five cats—and I finally look at my phone, thinking Ruben get to dinner get to dinner get to dinner and it's next week!

RUBEN *laughs wide.*

And oh, get this: apparently, at the penthouse party I choked this little Asian fashion designer guy, like nearly killed him because he wouldn't sing the Ovaltinies jingle with me.

'We are the itsy-bitsy teenie-weenie chockie malted Ovaltinies, made from Ovaltine and ready to crunch! We are the...'

You think you got me don't you. You think I'm one of you right?

You know what? I love 'blackouts'.

I think blackouts are a gift from god, he takes the details we care not to remember, and politely lifts them out of the brain, so we wake up, and all we can recall is heading out and coming home—it's *nice*—of GOD.

1.4: SUBLIMINAL AGENCY

RAY: Morning Hendrix!

How is my Golden Boy?

Latte latte latte latte!

RUBEN: You got four coffees Ray?

RAY: One for each man in the room and one for each... Creative!

You ok Chopin?

RUBEN: Yeah, I'm cool—just haven't been sleeping.

RAY: The curse of the active mind ey?

RUBEN: Did you have insomnia when you gave up the booze Ray?

RAY: Can't remember!

RUBEN: You were a bit of a clown on the sauce weren't you Ray?

Didn't you go to gaol for like

RAY: This new Xtra Light Wheat Beer ad!

What have you got? Did you read the sheet?

RUBEN: Which?

I didn't see...

RAY: About beer and women.

Pointing beer at women!

RUBEN: I just want to know if you slept well when you…

RAY: Mate, ok, I love you like a son, but seriously of late you've been no use to me.

Lope in here all depressing.

Falling asleep at your G5, gazing out the window like some kind of stoned teenager.

RUBEN: Zoya left me.

RAY: Yeah, I know, you've talked about that and I believe that would be… *Hard!*

That's admittedly, I agree, that'd not be easy—she's *very…* skinny.

RUBEN: Why can't you talk about these things with me Ray?

You've been through it; I'm going through it now.

RAY: Because I don't care.

RUBEN: You don't care about my drinking problem??

RAY: Metro-sexuals destroying everything our ancestors built up with your fucken caring and feeling—look!

It's not easy—the *booze* thing.

RUBEN: No.

RAY: So.

Good luck.

RUBEN: That's it?

RAY: I said good luck!

RUBEN: I have a problem Ray!

RAY: Well so do I!

RUBEN: Let us share!

RAY: And it's called Xtra Light Wheat Beer!

RUBEN: I can't sell beer Ray.

In the headspace I'm in.

RAY: I'm sure I keep a shotgun round here somewhere.

/Where is it?

TABATHA!

RUBEN: /Like I've suddenly stopped and all the horrid shit I did is reeling back in front of me.

Snorting cocaine in churches, pouring vodka in my granola, orgies with fifteen-year-old soap stars in hotels.

RAY: Which soap?

RUBEN *sings the opening line of the 'Home and Away' theme.*

I gotta' get out more.

RUBEN: I've been doing this shit Ray the whole time I've been working at Subliminal, and the whole time I've been doing it I've been engaged to the most beautiful girl.

RAY: Ok. I'm going to be honest with you Thorpie.

You're the most talented Creative Director Subliminal has ever had, *ever.*

Every pitch, every concept, every platform you build—make a lot of noise.

And don't think for a second Subliminal don't know it.

But! If you keep wandering round here in your teetotalling daze of self-flagellation then Subliminal suffers. And if Subliminal suffers September 11 type shit.

On my head. Ray's *head.* 9-11 type shit.

So, I suggest you go over there and do exactly what we BOTH KNOW you need to do to get that mojo back in range because I'm not losing my big fat harbour-view office just because you had a couple of tiffs with the supermodel, ok?

RUBEN: What have I got to do Ray?

Enlighten me.

RAY *issues* RUBEN *a bottle of vodka.*

You think the only way I can do this job is drunk Ray?

RAY: Since you've been in the program your ideas have been sub-standard AT BEST and Subliminal are asking me why.

I mean the tampon ad pitch, with the girl on the desert island?

Is it 1983 outside?

RUBEN: That was about Purity.

About a girl searching for *Purity.*

RAY: You've lost your fucking edge boy!

It's cool—it happened to me when I switched to Earl Grey, it's natural.

But I'm an Executive—you're a Creative!

RUBEN: Ok. Ok.

I'll drink the bottle of vodka.

RAY: Good news.

RUBEN: If you drink it with me.

Why not Ray? Because you have a 'Problem with Alcohol'?

What happened that night Ray? What made you…

RAY: Tabatha!

RUBEN: Pathetic.

RAY: You just keep in your corner boy or I will come down on you so hard you won't know what fucken hit you, alright?

RUBEN: I'm not drinking Ray. Not for you, not for Subliminal, not for anyone. I'm getting my fiancée back and that's pretty much all I care about.

RAY: Ok, I can roger that.

RUBEN: I'm glad.

Now, I'm off to my 'Opening the Big Black Door' meeting.

RAY: All the best with it.

RUBEN: Want to come?

RAY: I'll meet you there.

I just gotta make a phone call to The Board.

Tell them you'll be taking lesser duties creatively.

Now that you've got all these 'Personal Nourishment' meetings to go to.

Make Ruben Guthrie more of a side player.

You'll have time on your hands.

Time on your own.

Plenty of time to just.

Be on your own.

With your *headspace.*

Long pause.

RUBEN: Picture the most fascinating twenty-two-year-old girl you have ever seen. In a tight singlet.

Tears streaming down her face and onto her small cleavage.

CUE: Death Cab For Cutie—*Translanticism*—BAM!

Pull back, reveal:

She and her boyfriend are having this enormous fight—it's a break-up.

So emotional—like some amazing cable drama.

He breaks down in the lounge room, scratching at his own face.

She hurls his stuff at him—the broken portrait on the floor.

So much pain.

She loves him *so* much.

He loves *her so* much.

But she throws him out of the house, after the most INTENSE goodbye kiss.

She walks back into the kitchen, so sad, sobbing and sweating into her singlet.

She opens the fridge.

Pulls out an Xtra Light Wheat Beer.

Cracks it open.

Slams it down.

And feels… *Powerful.*

Again.

X Wheat Beer.

Yes, it hurts.

RAY *is crying?*

RAY: And that's why Ruben Guthrie is the best.

How do you feel Ruben?

RUBEN: How do I feel? I don't know. How do you feel Ray?

RAY: How do I feel?

'I feel like a Tooheys! I feel like a Tooheys! I feel like a Tooheys or two!'

How about you?!

1.5: A HALL

RUBEN: School school school school school.

Fuck, um—well my parents sent me to a boarding school. I mean how hard is it to have one kid asleep at night in your house how hard is it but no… *boarding school!*

Look, I gotta say I wasn't like 'this' at boarding school, I didn't like getting smashed on rocket fuel and talking about vaginas, honestly I had no interest in Alcohol at all.

I spent my money on magazines and electronics—fashion mostly. By the time I reached Year Eight I had fifteen pairs of jeans.

So of course the rugby guys and the rowing guys and the wrestling guys would come in at night and they'd pin me down and get it out of their system—the *rage.*

'Nice shoes faggot—you got mousse in your hair let's put mousse in his anus!'

I'd be flipping through *Mad* magazine and just put the thing down and take it.

Fine.

But then this guy called Corey joined our school, and suddenly all that stopped.

Corey was older than me, bigger than me and a whole lot cooler than me. He drove a black Suzuki Vitara had five earrings and the word 'Fuck' tattooed inside his lip. My mum was always saying 'bring Corey with you on the weekend' and she'd go all flushed and wear low-cut tops in the kitchen.

To this day I don't know why he chose me but he did.

The first day he arrived he saw the way it was for me in that place and he... made it go away. He'd look after me and I'd tell him my thoughts on things my story ideas, we were inseparable we were... *Close.*

Corey repeated Year Twelve then he was kicked out and so his dad got him a job bending corrugated iron in a factory but by then he was... he was deep into drugs and not good drugs, like seedy eight-balls—we never lost contact but we lost... *flow.*

Corey called me up one night at college said he needed a friend.

Said he was sick of speed and bending corrugated iron his voice was thin it was hollow.

He said he needed a *real mate* and I was the only *real mate* he had.

He was crying on the phone.

I'd never heard Corey cry I never imagined Corey *could* cry.

There was a party on in our house at college, a big party and Damian and my lip-sync band were playing.

I said I'd call him back tomorrow for a big chat—told him to not look into things so much. To chill out, I said—I said 'chill out Corey', laughed and hung up.

I didn't call back I forgot I just clean forgot I was so... *consumed* by my new world.

They found him in his dad's boat in the garage, he was...

From then on I started to like drinks a lot, liked the taste of them in my mouth, the burn of them in my ribs, the zing and jolt of Alcohol in my blood in my brain.

I thought.

If he's gone.
Then I'll just drink.
And drink…
And drink…

1.6: A BACK DECK

PETER: Red wine.
RUBEN: Ahh—
PETER: White wine?
RUBEN: No thanks Dad.
PETER: Ice-cold beer?
RUBEN: Do you have any mineral water on hand?
PETER: It's a thirty-degree day, Sun Ye's got prawns marinating, and you
    want a glass of water?
RUBEN: Yes.
PETER: You hung over? Always hung over when you see me—never save
    yourself.
RUBEN: I'm not hung over at all Dad.
    I was at the gym at six a.m.
PETER: Yeah? I was at aqua-aerobics!

> PETER *laughs. Thinks* RUBEN *was joking too. Hands* RUBEN *a glass
> of wine.* RUBEN *doesn't take it.*

RUBEN: Just a water then, thanks Dad.
    A water? Please—
PETER: Water, water, water yes clean the palate good thoughts.
    Sun Ye! Get Ruben a water will you?!
RUBEN: Does Sun Ye own this place?
PETER: Yeah! Not bad ey, for a New Australian.
    Speaking of: where is Zoya?
RUBEN: Munich Dad, I told you on the phone.
PETER: Alright. Don't attack me.
RUBEN: I wasn't attacking you.
PETER: Alright then. Good. Let's all get on well then.
    You going to visit her? Munich?
RUBEN: Oh yeah, of course I am!
    I mean… Zoya really wants me to be with her.
    Kind of begging me to fly over *now!*

PETER: Gorgeous girl that one.

> Zoya.
>
> Very fit, very attractive.
>
> Very very—*nubile* looking girl.

RUBEN: *Nubile?*

PETER: I mean you've done well keeping a piece like her on deck all this time.

RUBEN: I'm Creative Director of Subliminal Dad.

> I'm Head *Writer.*
>
> What? Why are you laughing?

PETER: You make ads.

RUBEN: Yes, I'm Creative Director of—

PETER: *Jingles* and *Ads.*

> And don't think you can go calling yourself a writer; John Grisham is a writer.
>
> How's your mother?

RUBEN: Dead.

PETER: What?

> She's not!

RUBEN: Call her up and find out.

PETER: Why are you being such a cock-smoker? I ask you over…

RUBEN: How do you think she is Dad? One minute you're in the kitchen the next you're moving in with the Asian chick from the restaurant, I mean…

PETER: Don't talk about Sun Ye like she's…

RUBEN: Like she's what?

PETER: How's the arm?

RUBEN: Great thanks Daddy!

> PETER *comes at* RUBEN *with the glass of wine.*

PETER: Righto then. Let's get pissed and catch up.

RUBEN: Dad, really, water is…

PETER: Get it into ya!

RUBEN: No!

> RUBEN *pushes the glass away and red wine spills on* PETER*'s shirt.*

PETER: Fuck *me!* Fuck.

> Just trying to enjoy each other's company.
>
> Trying to BOND with my fucken SON who I'm PROUD of.
>
> I may fast forward the ads but I'm proud of you.

RUBEN: /She left me Dad.

PETER: /Me good shirt. Who left?

RUBEN: *Zoya* left me.

PETER: Because of the jumping off the hotel thing?

      Or the gone missing thing?

      Or the drink drive chase thing?

RUBEN: None of them specifically but…

PETER: I've told you before, if you're going to drink and drive, do it at peak hour.

RUBEN: That wasn't it Dad, she…

PETER: Oh, what she found another bloke?

      She having an affair on you was she?

RUBEN: No, she…

PETER: Men get the blame for all that shit, but I'll give you the drum, there's a lot of wandering pussy out there my friend! Believe you me! *Wandering pussy.*

RUBEN: Zoya.

      She left me because of my.

      Problem.

      With.

      Alcohol.

PETER: She *drinks.* I've seen her *drink.*

      Always enjoys a nice drink when *I* offer it to her?

RUBEN: Dad, what are you doing?

PETER: I'm on the back deck; it's a lovely summer's afternoon.

RUBEN: Dad, you're not listening to me.

      Mum doesn't know what happened.

      Mum doesn't know where you are.

PETER: She'll work it out.

RUBEN: Mum's at home and she's crying she's scared.

PETER: Yeah good, take your mother's side ONCE again.

RUBEN: But Dad she didn't…

PETER: We should go away again—you and I.

      Wine tasting in the Barossa Valley!

      I'll fucken fly us over all expenses on me.

      Remember when we did Margaret River?

RUBEN: Dad I'm.

      I.

I'm struggling with it.

Well no I lost the struggle, battle.

I'm not saying it's genetic or whatever but it's a disease and I'm making connections with other people to grow stronger.

If you ever wanted to come and talk about it.

With us. There's a group.

On Mondays.

For dads and sons, who—

You don't have to share or anything, just be there and…

PETER: Get!

END OF ACT ONE

ACT TWO

2.1: STREET OUTSIDE HALL

VIRGINIA: Do you smoke?

RUBEN: No, yes, no.

I don't have any, if that's, was that what you…

VIRGINIA: It's ok.

RUBEN: I did *smoke*.

I have *smoked*.

I *smoke*.

But I'm not *smoking*.

VIRGINIA: I just need a lighter dude.

RUBEN: I wish I smoked.

VIRGINIA: You should smoke.

RUBEN: What? Why?

VIRGINIA: You look tense.

RUBEN: Do I?

VIRGINIA: Yes.

Very.

RUBEN: I can't sleep.

Ever since I stopped, can't sleep a wink.

VIRGINIA: You should come swimming with me some time.

RUBEN: Sure.

VIRGINIA: You don't have to…

RUBEN: I'm not much of a swimmer, but sure if…

VIRGINIA: The only reason I asked you is because you get an ionic exchange of electrical energy from your synapses meeting with the water, which when night comes, takes the fire out of your body and allows it to give in to the unconscious and sleep.

RUBEN: Is that right?

VIRGINIA: Yep.

RUBEN: Wow.

> *Pause.*

VIRGINIA: Do you want to get a coffee Ruben?

RUBEN: YES!

VIRGINIA: Whoah.

RUBEN: I mean, no.

VIRGINIA: No?

RUBEN: I don't drink coffee.

> A lot.

VIRGINIA: Ok…

RUBEN: During the week.

VIRGINIA: You should.

RUBEN: Why?

VIRGINIA: Cigarettes.

> Coffee.

> It's all we have left.

RUBEN: But doesn't that defeat the purpose?

VIRGINIA: Of what?

RUBEN: Giving up say Alcohol?

VIRGINIA: Speed as well.

RUBEN: Oh, you, yeah you—

VIRGINIA: I'm an addict, yes. Six years clean.

RUBEN: Well done. /'One day at a time!'

VIRGINIA: /'One day at a time!'

> *They laugh together.*

RUBEN: Right. So, we do this so we don't die.

> Give up our respective vices, go to meetings, work through the steps; face the demons.

VIRGINIA: Yep.

RUBEN: Self-loathing, make amends, embrace the *pain*.

VIRGINIA: Yes.

RUBEN: And then we smoke. Which kills us! I don't see how…

VIRGINIA: I'm just saying give yourself six months and smoke a bit, don't think you got to be Mr *Pure* just because you're Dry and Sharing.

Go easy on yourself.

RUBEN: How long are you going to smoke for?

VIRGINIA: Forever.

RUBEN: Right. No, good choice.

VIRGINIA: But I'm not like you, I don't have a mortgage and a relationship.

RUBEN: How did you…

You're not in a?

You don't have…

VIRGINIA: I just have *me*.

And my hell.

And no lighter.

RUBEN: Let's grab a coffee.

VIRGINIA: No.

RUBEN: But you said, just before—

VIRGINIA: Talking to you makes me want to Use.

RUBEN: Shit, I didn't mean to…

VIRGINIA: It's ok, it's a compliment.

Pause.

Bye Ruben.

VIRGINIA *goes.*

RUBEN: I didn't catch your—

2.2: A KITCHEN

ZOYA: Hi you've reached Zoya on the phone, please leave a message and I will definitely get back to you. Have a *great* day Hombre.

RUBEN: Zoya, it's me, calling.

Again.

Starting to feel like a stalker.

Your voice message says you'll 'definitely call back' you might want to look at that.

OR just call back and leave the message how it is.

Mum's just here at the house.

We read that it's really cold in the Czech Republic now, snow and all.

I know you love the snow so you're probably happy with that!

Wish I could see it. And you in a puffy jacket!

I'm on Step Two now at Group Meeting! It's going really well, it's really scary babe.

I'm better now because of it, but it's terrifying.

Just call me when you can, I've got so much I want to Share.

MUM: Maybe they don't have mobile range in Czechoslovakia.

RUBEN: I just want to talk to her Mum!

I know I've been appalling—I know that.

But I'm working so hard on myself, the least she could do is call?

Thanks for coming over with my washing.

You've been such an incredible support through my recovery.

MUM: Oh, you were an awful drunk.

RUBEN: Mum, don't…

MUM: At your Nanna's eightieth when you pissed in the restaurant plants.

RUBEN: Ok, do we have to go into this?

MUM: Shoved your pubic hair in Auntie Gale's face.

RUBEN: I was just comparing her mohair scarf with my…

MUM: Last Christmas Day when you dropped little Dorian on his head.

RUBEN: I'd been at Dad's all afternoon!

MUM: That fool.

That.

Fool.

It takes two generations to clear Alcohol out of a family line.

Did you know that Ruben?

RUBEN: No, I didn't.

MUM: You're doing a good thing for your kids.

RUBEN: I'm just taking it 'one day at a time' Mum.

MUM: I know, but if you keep doing that for a few years, or forever—

RUBEN: Mum, I can't pressure myself with forever. I'm only meant to think about getting through *today.*

MUM: Sure, but if you get through *today,* surely you can make plans for a group of days, or a year of days, and if—

RUBEN: The saying is 'one day at a time' Mum!

MUM: I don't think that's particularly ambitious do you? 'One day at a time'?

RUBEN: I'm going for a swim.

Helps me sleep because of the ionic exchange… the synapses.

MUM: Why don't I move in with you for a while?

Both of us have been abandoned and I can help you with the house.

Your father took the car—I don't have a car anymore Ruben.

I don't necessarily feel safe on my own in a big place.

I had to walk to the IGA the other night and this horrible man I thought 'he's going to kill me' and the little security guard won't stop him.

This man he spat black spit at me I tell you these people these hateful people.

I don't feel safe and none of the girls at the restaurant like me they all whisper I can hear.

I'm not shopping at the IGA anymore even though it's just down the street I can't shop there it's not safe I don't feel safe at all Ruben!

Ruben, I don't have a car I'm your mother and everyone's turned against me.

Ruben?

RUBEN: I went to this 'Touching Yesterday's Pain' meeting last night. And they talked about how Alcohol is genetic. Like inherited. And I'm sitting there thinking: well obviously!

MUM: Ruben am I that atrocious am I boring?

I'm not quick and pleasant anymore.

RUBEN: I sat there thinking hard and deep—listening fierce about it.

Wondering if what you inherit *is* this 'disease', this chemical imbalance that creates a need for the substance. If it's as simple as that. Inheriting a 'disease'. Or is what you're inheriting deeper than that? Are you actually inheriting generations of *pain*? Or shame or insecurity or shyness or guilt? And that's why you drink like your ancestors because you have the same void, the same black hole; the same demons to suppress. Is that what it means? A 'genetic illness'? When you're passed down, in some black emotional package that you have no choice but to accept; all your parents' guilt, everything your parents /failed to…

*/*MUM *leaves.*

That went well.

  MUM *re-enters.*

MUM: You say what you like about Peter and myself but you'll soon find out it's the drink it's the drink Ruben it's the drink and no-one steps in and says no more drinking no-one steps in and says that's enough no-one steps in because you're all too bloody scared to go without. My father had everything and he threw it all away because the drink it's the drink and... NOW... thirty-five years of marriage and your father runs off with some... YOUNG... and you know why Ruben? She pours him drinks! She keeps quiet and serves her master with a nice cool drink. It's drink. It's the drink.

  MUM *leaves.* RUBEN *sings 'Toy Soldiers'.*

RUBEN: *It wasn't my intention to mislead you. It never should have been this way. What can I say? It's true, I did extend the invitation, I never knew how long you'd stay...*

  DAMIAN *enters with a suitcases and duty free bags of booze.*

DAMIAN: *When you hear temptation call It's your heart that takes, takes a fall*

RUBEN: *Won't you come out and play with me /Step by step, heart to heart, left right left We all fall down... (all fall down)... like Toy Soldiers...*

DAMIAN: */Step by step, heart to heart, left right left We all fall down... (all fall down)... like Toy Soldiers...*

RUBEN: Damian. D-Love!

  What the fuck??

DAMIAN: */Bit by bit... torn apart... we never win... (but the battle wages on...)*

RUBEN: /Stop with the Martika man, what are you doing in my house?!

DAMIAN: I know, right?

  I can hardly believe it either. Now just before we unfurl: May I doss my gay arse down at yours for a couple or what?

RUBEN: Oh. Um.

DAMIAN: 'Um'?

RUBEN: What do you mean? Of course man! What the fuck!

  They hug. DAMIAN *is soon unloading booze onto the kitchen table.*

DAMIAN: I'll explain. Lots to explain, Damian will explain, just need to fix me a tall glass of something flammable. The fucking mediocre booze they make you drink on the plane!

    Dry white wine does one think?

    Draa whaa waaaaaa!

    It is only morning time.

RUBEN: I'm off the sauce man.

DAMIAN: Ha!

RUBEN: No more booze.

    Damian serious.

DAMIAN: Is this you listening to that anorexic Czech of yours again?

RUBEN: Off my own bat.

DAMIAN: Get off tomorrow!

    For now we get cunted old-style.

RUBEN: Damian, I'm seriously *sober.*

    I've been sober for—

DAMIAN: Ruben.

    I love you—I haven't seen you in two and a half months and I love you.

    I want to drink all this untaxed booze with you.

    Please, don't tell me I cannot express my love to you in the way that we know best?

    Yeah baby, come on baby.

RUBEN: What booze did you get?

DAMIAN: Duty free Sancerre, ahhhhhhhh Schnapps, vodka, single malt Glen, Bombay Sapphire, some absinthe and a filthy French red.

RUBEN: Margot?

DAMIAN: Nurf de Pap. 'Eighty-three.

RUBEN: I… I… I have a meeting.

    A step, stroke meeting.

DAMIAN: Meeting? Stroke…

RUBEN: At the pool!

    I'm meeting some other swimmers at the pool.

DAMIAN: Don't tell me you're sitting in a circle!

RUBEN: No!

DAMIAN: Are you?

RUBEN: Ok yes, I am!/

    And I really like it.

DAMIAN: /Noooooooooooo! They got you too!
  Evil evil Christian cunts!
RUBEN: Damian don't call them that—they save fucking lives man!
DAMIAN: Have you read *A Million Little Pieces*?!
RUBEN: Damian, what are you doing home?
  Two months ago we threw a going-away party for you, what happened to the 'New York job of a lifetime'!?
DAMIAN: Have a glass with me and I'll talk about it.
RUBEN: I have a meeting—
DAMIAN: One drink and I'll talk about it.
RUBEN: I'm going swimming.
DAMIAN: One!
RUBEN: If I have one—
DAMIAN: Have a drink!
RUBEN: No.
DAMIAN: Harmless.
RUBEN: D…
DAMIAN: Come on.
RUBEN: No.
DAMIAN: Yes.
RUBEN: No!
DAMIAN: Dude.
RUBEN: 'Dude'.
DAMIAN: Look who's back?
RUBEN: I said no /D-love.
DAMIAN: /Just the one!
RUBEN: What did I say?
DAMIAN: Sip sip mm-mmm.
RUBEN: Jesus.
DAMIAN: I'll pour.
RUBEN: Didn't you hear me?
DAMIAN: I heard you—
RUBEN: Good!
DAMIAN: One drink!
RUBEN: You know what'll happen if we…
DAMIAN: We don't have to have ten—just have one.
RUBEN: When did we *ever* have one?
DAMIAN: Ok, let's have ten!

RUBEN: No!

DAMIAN: One?

RUBEN: Damian!

DAMIAN: One fucking glass! /Have a glass!

RUBEN: /You want a glass I'll put a glass in your face how do you feel about that for a glass you fucking faggot?! Huh, you want a glass in your eyeball? Huh?

> *Pause.*

DAMIAN: Oh my god.

> What did you just…

RUBEN: Sorry man.

> You needled me—don't needle me.

> DAMIAN *breaks down.*

Dame, sorry man—are you…

DAMIAN: The whole New York thing, I'm *so—*

RUBEN: Speak to me.

> About it.

> *Pause.* DAMIAN *gets a drink. Offers* RUBEN *one.* RUBEN *boils, then calmly says no.*

DAMIAN: —

> I had this idea.

> Related to Instant Messenger.

> Everyone in the office is on Instant Messenger right.

> Four hundred and forty of us.

> So I thought I'd invite everyone in the office to a group chat.

> Four hundred and forty people.

RUBEN: Nice idea.

DAMIAN: Ruben, it was incredible.

RUBEN: Sounds…

DAMIAN: Like better than any online feeling I've had before.

> The power of four hundred and forty people chatting at *once!*

> And everyone was amazed that I'd thought of it, and this was like, my third week or whatever and the Aaaaaaagency…

RUBEN: Stacked?

DAMIAN: Ohh Rubey!

RUBEN: Yeah?

DAMIAN: But then…

RUBEN: Uh-oh…

DAMIAN: I come back from lunch, and me and this other fag from Marketing'd been getting along really well right—and started this kinda friendly yet filthy chat relationship on Instant Messenger.

Kind of chat about what we'd like to do with different guys in the office blah blah blah.

Well I'm chatting to him online, on the work Messenger, and the chat gets pretty wrong pretty quickly, like I'm talking about bending the MD over the water cooler—

RUBEN: Here it comes.

DAMIAN: Fisting the MD, spit-roasting him with the black guy from Accounts!

RUBEN: Excellent!

DAMIAN: But what I didn't realise…

RUBEN: Four hundred and forty.

DAMIAN: Four hundred and forty people.

RUBEN: You were on GROUP!

DAMIAN: Group Chat baby!

/Talking about anally and orally ROASTING the Managing Director—on Group Chat!

RUBEN: /Noooooooooooooooooooooooooooooooo!

The wrath of I.M.

DAMIAN: And I later find out, as I'm being escorted from the building— that he's married with kids but was once sprung in the lifts with a Mexican boy. /But no it's all my fault!

RUBEN: /Ohh mate.

Great way to go though; /the story…

DAMIAN: /*So* good to see you again—I missed you Ruben Guthrie.

Can I stay here with you and all these lovely pretty shiny bottles?

DAMIAN *kisses* RUBEN *and goes.*

2.3: SUBLIMINAL AGENCY

RAY *enters. Singing.*

RAY: *My dad picks the fruit that goes to Cottees! To make the cordial— that I like best!*

Sing it with me!

Aussie kids, are Weet-Bix kids, I said Aussie kids, are Weet—Bix— kids!

Or our special little favourite duet!

They count each other in. They could do the 'happy family' actions. Making cakes and sipping drinks like they do in the 1990 TV advertisement!

So Good on your cakes and your biscuits.

RUBEN: *So Good!*

RAY: *So Good in your puddings and pies.*

RUBEN: *So Good!*

RAY: *So Good on your cereal…*

RUBEN: *So Good as a drink.*

RAY & RUBEN: *So Good is the reason why… So Good is so good!*

Drum break.

RAY: *No cholesterol.*

RUBEN: *No lactose.*

RAY: *That's another reason to try…*

RAY & RUBEN: *Sanitarium So Goooooodddd…!*

RAY: So! The big guns are releasing a brand *new* pre-mix vodka drink for young girls, y'know the deal: pumped full of booze and sugar so the sixteen-year-old girls can slam down five in an hour 'cos they *'just can't believe how nice it tastes!'* And then they toddle off to the toilet but for some reason they trip over their barstool and onto the floor of the nightclub they go! With their legs akimbo and their *fresh* little *wet* little twats in the air for all to see!

What was the one that started it all?

RUBEN: Sub Zero.

RAY: Bingo!

RUBEN: With *grenadine.*

RAY: Similar vibe here, sexy thin bottle a selection of citrus flavours slimming yet fun—they want a 'flashy-aggressive yet *sexy* Paris Hilton on a horse' type advert—/hit me!

RUBEN: /Ray.

RAY: Shall we sing?

Good on ya' Mum…

RUBEN: Please, no more iconic Australian jingles.

RAY: My first thoughts just out of my head: Really toned Latino guys

between fourteen and twenty-one. Dancing with these big white
pandas in a glass maze and then a new batch of pandas fall from the
sky and the Latino guys are like looking up mouthing 'check out the
new pandas!'

RUBEN: Sit down Ray.

> I want to talk to you.

RAY: What? What's that look in your eye?

> /Novak?

> RUBEN *just goes for it.*

RUBEN: /You've been like a dad to me Ray.

RAY: Oh no no no no no, don't you fuck with me Federer!

RUBEN: Where I'm at now, with the meetings. I've had to swallow my
pride and admit that *I*, like *you*, have to spend the rest of my days
without liquor.

RAY: Roger me.

RUBEN: To do all this, to face all this, I have admitted that there is a
power greater than me.

RAY: Yes, yes, I remember the stings.

RUBEN: *Beliefs* Ray.

RAY: I never thought I'd see the day where a smart bloke like you, fell
for the 'poor me Christian tricks'.

RUBEN: The movement is not a trick Ray, it's—

RAY: Oh fucken wake up Roger they prey on guys like you—they turn
your love for the booze into a love of talking about yourself and pretty
soon you're spouting empty mantras like /'power greater than me'!

RUBEN: /I can't make ads anymore Ray, they're a symptom of my fear,
I—

RAY: 'Fear —fear—fear'! World's most overused word. FEAR!

RUBEN: I always wanted to be a writer, a novelist, but instead I make
ads! I hide behind this job Ray, behind the luxury of it, the facade—
the delusion!

RAY: Suck me off.

RUBEN: I'm hiding Ray.

> In this big brassy office buzzing with /ads and brands I'm hiding
/and so are you!

RAY: /How long do you want?

> A month?

Take two months off. Paid.

//Paid!

RUBEN: //I quit Ray.

I quit.

Sobriety First.

RAY: Negh!

RUBEN: It'll eat away at you Ray.

/It'll eat you from the inside.

//Ray I can help you.

RAY: /For your own safety get out of this office.

//For your own safety leave now.

RUBEN: Find your son Ray.

RAY: Get a box…

RUBEN: Atone.

RAY: Fill it up—and fuck off!

RUBEN: Ray.

RAY: I said now!

2.4: ZOYA & RUBEN'S PLACE

Sex.

VIRGINIA: Now!

RUBEN: Now!?

VIRGINIA: Are you. Oh. There.

RUBEN: Are you? Oh. Get. Phdd. Yes.

VIRGINIA: If you are?

RUBEN: YES? ARE YOU?

VIRGINIA: Oh yes! Now-wow. Now!

RUBEN: Donkld! Sutt—phwoah!

RUBEN *cums.*

By the Power of Greyskull!

VIRGINIA: Did you cum?

RUBEN: Yeah! Hoo.

And you'??

VIRGINIA: No.

Almost.

RUBEN: But you said you were about to!

VIRGINIA: It's ok pumpkin.

> You'll make me cum hundreds of times.

> Your forehead just changed.

RUBEN: No, it didn't.

VIRGINIA: Was that too full-on?

> Am I being too full-on?

RUBEN: No, I'm just.

> I only came because you said.

> You did say that you were about to!

> VIRGINIA *gets up and out.*

What are you doing?

VIRGINIA: Ohhh, I feel, breath—this is…

RUBEN: This is…?

VIRGINIA: I just, I thought I was ready for sex and I'm not.

> It triggered panic in me, and…

RUBEN: We've been fucking every day for like—

VIRGINIA: It's very personal to me ok?

> It's not just *fucking* ok?

RUBEN: Ok.

> Sorry.

VIRGINIA: Sorry.

RUBEN: I'm sorry.

VIRGINIA: No 'I feel' sorry.

RUBEN: Ok.

VIRGINIA: When I Used.

> I'd get so messed up in bars and go right up to guys.

> Divorced guys with kids at home—guys you see and you know you shouldn't.

> I'd go back to his place and suddenly I'd be like 'no', and he'd be like 'sorry yes'…

RUBEN: Oh V…

VIRGINIA: And I'd Drink and Use, like these guys were just one of three parts.

> And now I'm fucking again, my body is asking where the other two are?

> And it makes me *want* them. *Involved.*

> I feel so *vulnerable* and *unsafe* right now.

> VIRGINIA *picks a t-shirt out a drawer.*

RUBEN: Ahh, that's Zoya's t-shirt.

VIRGINIA: —

    May I?!

RUBEN: Ummmmm… sure!

    VIRGINIA *puts Zoya's t-shirt on.*

VIRGINIA: Do you think of Zoya when we're fucking?

RUBEN: No.

VIRGINIA: Honestly?

RUBEN: Now you're wearing her t-shirt I'm thinking about her, but…

    Zoya and I.

    It wasn't always about sex. By the end, it—

VIRGINIA: So what you're saying is you didn't connect sexually like we do?

    I'll go.

    VIRGINIA *goes to go.*

RUBEN: I didn't say *go*, I just said…

VIRGINIA: Sorry.

    I stepped over the line.

    I always step over the line when I'm feeling… stop saying 'feeling' Virginia!

    What's that smile?

    Stop it, you're embarrassing me!

RUBEN: Zoya put up with me for three years while I was a monster.

    And I will always love and respect her for that.

    But she never wanted to know me like you do.

    You even like what's wrong with me.

VIRGINIA: Feel like we found each other.

RUBEN: Like two little broken birds that helped put each other's wings back on again.

VIRGINIA: Tweet-tweet!

    They start making bird noises. Touching.

  Ruben!

RUBEN: If you don't want to have sex again that's fine! I don't want to trigger anything in you!

VIRGINIA: I've been evicted Ruben. They're knocking my building down and turning it into a Dan Murphy Liquor Warehouse.

RUBEN: Stay here.

VIRGINIA: No!

RUBEN: Yes, of course stay here.

VIRGINIA: No, I wasn't suggesting…

RUBEN: Well, *I* am!

VIRGINIA: If the Program find out we're living together!

RUBEN: I'll talk to Janine—

VIRGINIA: I can't live here.

Not with Damian… he drinks all day I can't be around—

RUBEN: V…

VIRGINIA: I *can't!*

Damian.

He'll trigger…

RUBEN: He's my best friend.

Virginia?

Where are you off to?

VIRGINIA: I'm going to a meeting because I feel unhinged and dis-combobulated.

It's because you make me feel beautiful and I'm still not comfortable feeling that way.

RUBEN: Why are girls these days so uncomfortable with being beautiful?!

VIRGINIA *goes to him. They hug and dance in a circle.*

2.5: ZOYA & RUBEN'S PLACE

DAMIAN *enters singing George Michael's* Faith. *He continues singing the song intermittently throughout the scene as indicated.*

RUBEN: How's the job hunting going D-Love?

DAMIAN: What a fucking hassle!

I started looking online but then I just ended up on Gaydar again.

RUBEN: Because I thought maybe you could apply for my job.

I shot an email off today, Ray wants to meet you.

DAMIAN: Dude, what do you take me for?

RUBEN: What?

DAMIAN: I'm not taking—I'm not *replacing* you.

RUBEN: Why not?

DAMIAN: 'Why not'?

RUBEN: I don't care, seriously.

I'd prefer it was you.

> DAMIAN *sings another line of 'Faith'.*

Is what you're drinking from my cellar?

DAMIAN: This Californian zinfandel is fucking dreamy!

> VIRGINIA *comes out with some settings for dinner.*

VIRGINIA: Hi Damian!

DAMIAN: Hi Vir—gin—ia!

VIRGINIA: How are you?

DAMIAN: I'm so great how are you?

VIRGINIA: Fantastic!

DAMIAN: That's fantastic! Wow!

VIRGINIA: Wow what?

DAMIAN: Just wow!

VIRGINIA: Ok!

DAMIAN: Woo!

VIRGINIA: Right!

> DAMIAN *sings another line of 'Faith'.*

VIRGINIA: Ruben!

> DAMIAN *sings another line of 'Faith'.*

Ruben!

RUBEN: [*over the next line of Damian's singing*] /Yes! What? Who?

> DAMIAN *sings the last line before the first chorus of 'Faith'.*

VIRGINIA: You were going to say to Damian about that thing!

DAMIAN: Going to say what about what thing?

RUBEN: Let's just eat the sausages first—mmmmm sausage!

VIRGINIA: You said you were going to say a thing—

DAMIAN: What were you going to say Ruben 'a thing'?

RUBEN: Where are those sausages man?

VIRGINIA: I'll get them while you say the thing to Damian!

RUBEN: The sausages…

DAMIAN: I'll get the sausages when the sausages are ready.

VIRGINIA: I'm happy to get them!

DAMIAN: They're my sausages!

VIRGINIA: We're all eating them!

DAMIAN: Sausage takes a while!

> *Pause.*

VIRGINIA: Ruben and I were talking about jobs and *living* and Ruben thought…

DAMIAN: So what do *you* do Virginia—to support the household?

Oh that's right, you just do the meetings! Do you get commission on recruitment?

VIRGINIA: Have you ever taken the quiz on the Alcoholics Anonymous website Damian?

DAMIAN: No! But I do like trawling Gaydar for cock.

VIRGINIA: There are ten questions and if you answer yes to four of them you're an Alcoholic.

DAMIAN: Four?

VIRGINIA: Just four.

DAMIAN: Are you guys low on attendance?

VIRGINIA: No, it's just an Honesty Test.

DAMIAN: I'm going to take it, I swear.

When I'm next online, if I can be fucking arsed, I may just log on.

VIRGINIA: I think you might get a sharp little wake-up call /Damian.

DAMIAN: /I went to an NA meeting once, and if it wasn't for the terminology, oh and Step Two, I probably would have returned. It felt like a pick-up joint though.

So, instead I went home and picked up my joint.

DAMIAN *takes a big sip of his wine, and then refills the glass.*

Have you ever fucked on E Virginia??

I love fucking on E.

You feel *everything.*

What's it like fucking on heroin? Or are you too *sleepy?*

VIRGINIA: I'm going to have a shower.

DAMIAN: Yeah, get nice and clean.

VIRGINIA *goes.*

She loves her showers man, how's your water bill—does she know there's a drought on?

RUBEN: How much of my collection have you demolished?

DAMIAN: Virginia told me to get rid of all your bottles. She said it was potentially 'dangerous' for you to have the 'demons' surrounding you in your 'sanctuary'.

RUBEN: That's several hundred dollars worth of booze and I expect you to pay me for it.

DAMIAN: You look skinnier today, you look really thin.

RUBEN: It's the no-job-no-fiancée-no-booze diet, you should try it.

DAMIAN: They say Alcoholics put on weight in the Program…

RUBEN: I'm not an Alcoholic Damian; I have a 'substance abuse problem' relating to—

DAMIAN: A glass of zinfandel for you then sir?

RUBEN: I can't have a glass Damian, seriously, think!

DAMIAN: But I thought you weren't an Alcoholic?

RUBEN: What the fuck are you treating her like that for?

DAMIAN: I didn't mean to offend the girl, if it wasn't so much fun I'd stop.

RUBEN: Her childhood is a litany of strange men at barbecues.

　She's had relatives put remote controls inside her.

　I'm just trying to help someone reach out.

DAMIAN: She's reaching out alright.

　All the way to your cock.

RUBEN: The spare room is taken now, where else is she going to sleep?!

DAMIAN: Ruben, admit it, she's fucking the shit out of you every night I can hear it thumping through the wall! Thundering symphony of two people who are so frustrated they can't get messed up, they're taking it all out on the mattress!

　DAMIAN *mimics* VIRGINIA*'s sex-talk.*

'Aaahg ughh ggrr fuck me I'm sober ahh fuckk I wish I could drink fourteen vodkas and shoot up! Fuck me agghhh yeah suck it ahhh *sobriety* ah!'

RUBEN: It's companionship is all, it's—

DAMIAN: Do you think your fiancée would see it that way?

　Long pause.

RUBEN: I love zinfandel.

　I really do.

　It's got *balls* zinfandel.

　But it's also got class.

　Not many wines have balls and class.

　Zinfandel does though.

DAMIAN: Remember when we performed 'Summer of '69' at the end-of-second-year party.

RUBEN: Yeah, I do.

DAMIAN: You were hot that night, so drunk and so hilarious in those black cut-off jean shorts, and your guitar pedal work and your vocal, the crowd were hailing you.

RUBEN: They were, weren't they?

> *Pause. He starts to sing Bryan Adams' 'Summer of '69'.*

DAMIAN: It's sad to think no-one will ever see that guy again.

> RUBEN *continues singing, and* DAMIAN *joins him.*

RUBEN: [*stopping as he gets to the end of the first verse*] How's the zinnie?

DAMIAN: Nothing short of mind-blowing: Reserve '81 so it's all ripe berries and smoky chocolate, the fruit is massive but the structure is delicate like you says—it is a truly cracking wine Ruben.

RUBEN: Pour me a fucking glass.

DAMIAN: Yeah baby!

> DAMIAN *pours a glass for* RUBEN *and himself. They assess the bouquet, swirl the wine round in the glass, and clink glasses.* DAMIAN *drinks from his glass.*

Are you going to drink that?

RUBEN: Virginia and I have been talking and it's really dangerous; potentially fatal really.

I mean look at what I'm holding Damian.

If you loved me you would not have let me go this far.

DAMIAN: I let you go that far because I do love you Ruben.

RUBEN: Virginia and I have decided that you can stay in the house and not drink, or leave the house and continue to drink.

What are you laughing at?

DAMIAN: She's Thirteenth Stepped you Ruben.

RUBEN: No she hasn't! What's that mean?

DAMIAN: She's made you need her like a Step, like you need all the other Steps.

RUBEN: That's not accurate.

DAMIAN: You poor Thirteenth-Stepped little faggot.

RUBEN: I think you should go now.

DAMIAN: You're getting rid of everything Ruben! For some rickety smack-head with daddy issues! Have a look around Ruben! Everything is walking away!

You're going to be on your own soon and we all know Ruben Guthrie doesn't like being on his own!

RUBEN: I'm working on strengthening my Alone Self!

DAMIAN: Stop with the sound bites just for a fucking second.
    I am your best friend and I am scared for you!

RUBEN: I'd like you to leave now.

DAMIAN: Ruben, can you hear me? You're in danger!

RUBEN: Please leave Damian.

DAMIAN: Why are you doing this to yourself Ruben? Why are you doing this to *me*?

RUBEN: Because we are not the same.

> DAMIAN *goes into his room.*
>
> VIRGINIA *comes out in a towel. She puts her arms around* RUBEN.
>
> DAMIAN *comes back in with his luggage and a sausage in his mouth.*
>
> DAMIAN *exits with his stuff, taking the bottle of zinfandel with him.*
>
> VIRGINIA *kisses* RUBEN *and exits back into the bedroom, drying her hair.*
>
> RUBEN *stands alone on the stage. Isolated. Quietly and slowly, sings:*

Those were the best days of my life.

END OF ACT TWO

INTERVAL

ACT THREE

RUBEN: Hello my name is Ruben Guthrie and how exciting is this!? Hey...

I'm excited are you excited—this is the next level! We are blessed. Blessed to be sober and clean, and blessed to be here, on this special Saturday morning, in Centennial Park, with our dogs! Or in Janelle's case with her pig. I'm sorry Janelle what is that thing? Oh it's a pig-dog. Was that a rescue?

Thanks for responding so positively to this idea Group. I never thought I'd be standing here in the sunlight with you people but I gotta say it feels good. To have organised something with my Home Group I really. I'm chuffed. So thank you for the constant love and support.

Ken I think your Rottweiler is taking a shit on my rug. Ken you may want to...

What do you feed that thing?

It's... let's admit! It is fucking boring being sober. *Sometimes* Janelle sometimes!

It's the nights really isn't it? The days are ok because you feel so fresh, you don't have a hangover, and nothing clouds you—you're firing from the time you bounce out of bed; I'm alive I'm sober I'm drinking orange juice it's 6.05 in the morning and Mel and Koshie are my friends!

But then the night comes.

When you're drinking it's the days that feel heavy and the nights that sing. Stop drinking it's the days that sing songs and the night it just presses on your brain, it sticks needles in your eyes it makes pain in the middle of your chest it says 'drink' it says 'walk through the walls Ruben follow the lights Ruben follow the lights down the shiny road to the golden place'.

But I got you guys now. I got Janelle on the end of the phone I got Ken down the street with Guitar Hero but most of all I got the love of a good woman, a woman that says 'yes' to my problems and 'yes' to my trauma, and 'yes' to my ideas of buying a dog and calling it 'Pellegrino' and 'yes' to my idea of holding Saturday Group meetings in Centennial Park and sharing with our dogs our loyal canines and her name is Virginia and she gives me strength because she validates my pain, and that is why I am marrying her!

That girl over there with the puppy in her arms—she will be my wife!

My wife—my life.

RUBEN *howls into the wind.*

3.2: BACK DECK

PETER *has a glass of red.* RUBEN *has a tall bottle of sparkling mineral water.*

PETER: Mineral water good?

RUBEN: Yeah, so good I named my dog after it!

PETER: Don't—I would've let you bring him over but Sun Ye she gets scared of dogs. It's an Asian thing—they eat dog but they don't greet dog, it's...

RUBEN: So Dad, you said there was something pressing you had to tell me?

PETER: We used to have a hell of a time you and me.

Talking about white wines compare red wines...

RUBEN: My sponsor at the Movement...

PETER: 'The Movement'! Who are you: Che Guevara?

RUBEN: Virginia said that if it's too stressful coming here, then—

PETER: Look, if you want to get religious, think about this: Jesus Christ himself was a wine man. He took water, what you're drinking there, and turned it into wine, what I'm drinking here. That's what he did! Jesus himself, that's the way he arranged it.

RUBEN: Dad, why won't you respect my position?

PETER: Because you're *my* son!

Not some League player who gets pissed then rapes a fourteen-year-old in a carpark. You're just a normal guy who enjoys a normal couple of drinks!

RUBEN: I can't remain in this environment.

Emotionally.

PETER: Please stay son.

    Just I'm.

    Very stressed at the moment.

    What with work and the pancreatitis.

RUBEN: Pancreatitis?

    Dad? What the hell?

PETER: Pancreatitis is an inflammation of the pancreas, um. Yeah. *Not* good.

    And mine is apparently 'acute' and friggin' 'chronic' or some other.

    Getting this pain in my back, nails—and yeah, vomiting a bit, jaundice of the ahh... the skin so yeah um... friggin' went in—tests!

RUBEN: When did you start feeling pain?

PETER: Couple of years ago.

RUBEN: Why didn't you go to the doctor?

PETER: I went last week!

        PETER *turns on* RUBEN.

And so better you Ruben! When you're forty get your fucken tests don't be an idiot and leave it till it's too late alright?!

RUBEN: Ok Dad—but Dad isn't pancreatitis to do with excessive drinking?

PETER: *Trauma.*

    Stress and trauma.

    You've got no idea what it's like running a restaurant, a 'hat' restaurant, and you may have noticed the Floor Manager no longer comes in.

RUBEN: Oh, your wife... is that who you're talking about?

PETER: Don't get married Ruben.

    It's not natural for us men.

    We're built to conquer and we're built to wander.

RUBEN: Dad, are—

    Dad, are you going to die?

PETER: Sun Ye and I. There's not a lot to discuss. She can't say much anyway. And the pancreatitis... don't seem to be turning her on. Ha!

    Dunno what's happening at your house.

    Or if you're ever over at your mother's.

    Tell her I said hello, and that, if she wants to have a coffee or—

RUBEN: Dad. There is no way I—
PETER: Righto.
    I'm in for a sav blanc.

3.3

Beeeeeeeeep.

ZOYA: Hi you've reached Zoya on the phone, please leave a message and
    I will definitely try /and get back to you. Have a *great* day!
RUBEN: / [*eyebrow raised*] Hombre!
    Haven't heard from you still.
    Read the email you sent to Mum.
    Sounds interesting—the course and all.
    I sent you some flowers for your birthday.
    Sent them through interflora.com.cz.
    Not sure if they got there, and the note with them?
    Yeah, I didn't hear back so—not sure!
    I realised in 'Love, Hate and Other Feelings' Group today that I
blame you for a lot of things, and I'm trying to work through that.
    I would like to make amends with you and not just because it's
part of my homework but because I respect you Zoya. I don't think
I always did.
    The way you got up and left this house. Left this zoo and the
animal within it.
    Dad's sick.
    Zoya, my dad he might not…
    He's—
    You know what? Fuck you!
    I'm not sharing any of this with you.
    I fucking financed you for three years. I took you to the parties!
'Meet this hot new photographer! Meet this designer! Hip friends!
Here; Work visa! Rent-free waterfront apartment! Hybrid anyone?'
And now look at you! Run away as soon as things get a little messy,
as soon as the situation isn't perfect for Prague's favourite little leggy
princess she flies off home. Back to mummy! If you were here right
now I would not take a photo of you on my phone!
    I'm so lost babe.

I'm so alone.
And sometimes I just think…

3.4: RUBEN & ZOYA'S PLACE

VIRGINIA *enters.*

VIRGINIA: I am so exhausted!

RUBEN: Really? / 'Exhausted?'

VIRGINIA: /And I'm starving!

RUBEN: Mmm, see again. Are you really 'starving' or are just a bit hungry?

VIRGINIA: Dha?

RUBEN: I'm just saying, I think we should reserve the term starving for those who truly are starving and exhausted for those who have say… been at work all day?

VIRGINIA: Janelle called me today. Asked if you and I would be interested in organising the Annual Conference for Program this year.

RUBEN: 'Annual Conference'?

VIRGINIA: Annual Conference is when all Home Groups from the local area get together and Share and Talk and usually there's some music and maybe some *limbo*!

RUBEN: Limbo—look out!

VIRGINIA: That's why she thought you and I could organise it; spunk it up a little.

I mean everyone is so impressed with 'Dog Share Saturday'!

RUBEN: What do you have in mind?

VIRGINIA: Like you could write some funny sketches about the Program and I could cook my paella and drop some of my drum and bass records later on.

RUBEN: I haven't been to a meeting in almost a week.

VIRGINIA: *I'm* your meeting.

RUBEN: Step Thirteen.

VIRGINIA: What?

RUBEN: Nothing. Um! I've actually been thinking.

VIRGINIA: *Dangerous.*

RUBEN: Of writing a book.

Lately.

Virginia my dear.

VIRGINIA: My fiancée.

RUBEN: Yes, I'm really missing writing and I had an idea for a fiction novel.

VIRGINIA: What's the 'idea'?

VIRGINIA *does some beat-boxing.*

RUBEN: I don't know.

My experiences over the past few months.

VIRGINIA: You're not ready.

RUBEN: Excuse me?

VIRGINIA: You're not ready to write about your experiences.

You're only a fifth of the way through the fourth part of a twelve-step process.

RUBEN: Writing relaxes me!

I'm at my happiest when I'm writing.

VIRGINIA: 'Happiest'?

RUBEN: My *calmest* my most calm—you don't want me to write?

VIRGINIA: I never said 'I don't want you to write', on the contrary—I asked you to write a sketch for Conference, I *suggested* you write.

VIRGINIA *beat-boxes again.*

RUBEN: Why can't I write a book?

VIRGINIA: Look what happened when you last—

RUBEN: But I'm different now, I…

VIRGINIA: I'll tell you when you're different!

I think you should co-host Conference with me, and after that we'll de-brief with Janelle and decide whether you should take the book on.

As your Sponsor I think that's what you should do.

So let's just sit on the book for six to eight to eighteen months and look at it again then.

How does that sound? Ruben? My husband to be…

Kisses him.

I'm going to have a shower I am covered in soot.

RUBEN: Are you really? 'Covered'?

VIRGINIA *goes.*

Step by step, heart to heart, left right left, We all fall down (all fall down). Like Toy /Soldiers.

ZOYA *enters.*

ZOYA: */Soldiers...*

RUBEN: *Holy shit.* Zoya!

ZOYA: No, I'm an apparition.

RUBEN: How did you get in?

ZOYA: Key. Door. Turn.

RUBEN: This is happening!

ZOYA: I got the voice messages from you.

RUBEN: Did you? I must say I had no idea! One could've assumed they
    disappeared into a void!
        Into some Czechoslovakian abyss!

ZOYA: Shut up.

RUBEN: Ok.

ZOYA: I have heard you on the phone so many times coming down off the
    drugs, coming down off five-day bender, but I never hear this sound in
    your voice... this... heaviness...

RUBEN: You heard me?

ZOYA: And the Agency has some shoots for me to do.

RUBEN: Did you fly here for me or for the shoots?

ZOYA: I don't know yet Amigo.
        It looks different in here.

RUBEN: Yeah.

ZOYA: Who re-arranged all the things?

RUBEN: I did.

ZOYA: Scented candles?
        You can't stand any scented candles.

RUBEN: They grew on me... very quickly.

ZOYA: Is your dad ok?

RUBEN: He's got pancreatitis.

ZOYA: I couldn't get here any quicker Ruben, I'm studying!

RUBEN: I know, I know.

ZOYA: He's not dead yet is he?

RUBEN: No Zoya, he's not dead yet.
        Hopefully he won't be dead for a while.

ZOYA: So he's *not* dying?

RUBEN: If he manages to steer clear of Alcohol, cheese and stress he
    might live to a hundred.

ZOYA: Oh.

RUBEN: You sound disappointed.

ZOYA: No, I was just, your voicemail!

RUBEN: Did you miss me?

While you were away?

ZOYA: I did not miss you no; if anything I was breathing my own air again.

I was so young when you found me, I was sixteen and stupid naïve girl—I felt so flattered that this older amazing successful guy had chosen me—I never complained any bit of the things you did at night, all drunk and picking on me saying I had to do these things now I was with a man.

RUBEN: Zoy…

ZOYA: But then I am in the snow at home and I think of the things you have done for yourself.

So brave to give up drinking in this Alcoholic country, with this father you have and this job this world of vultures in the night say 'drink this come here take this drink' and so I think…

RUBEN: Zoya, I missed you so much.

ZOYA: If you hurt me again.

RUBEN: I couldn't if I tried.

ZOYA: What was that noise?

RUBEN: You have *got* to see the new restaurant up on the hill— /to die for!

ZOYA: /Ruben, who is in the shower?

Who bought the scented candles for the kitchen?

RUBEN: Let's jog to the restaurant!

Race ya!

RUBEN *jogs off.*

VIRGINIA: Hey Ruben!

Have I got a pimple on my back?

VIRGINIA *enters.*

Who?

ZOYA: Hello?

VIRGINIA: Hi! Sorry, I'm dripping everywhere.

ZOYA: Ok.

VIRGINIA: Virginia!

ZOYA: And you…

VIRGINIA: Me?

ZOYA: You are…

VIRGINIA: I'm Ruben's fi…

RUBEN *comes jogging back in.*

RUBEN: Virginia's landlord kicked her out of the house and since then I've been putting her up.

VIRGINIA: 'Putting me up'!

RUBEN: Zoya and I are going for a jog.

VIRGINIA: 'Zoya' Zoya?

ZOYA: Yes, my name is Zoya—I am Ruben's fiancée.

VIRGINIA: Excuse me?

RUBEN: She. We. See she we—

VIRGINIA: Ruben, I think it's important that Zoya learns of all the changes to the key relationships.

ZOYA: Yes Ruben, I want to learn of the key changes.

VIRGINIA: I'll just put some clothes on.

Make yourself at home.

ZOYA: This *is* my home.

VIRGINIA: Exactly!

VIRGINIA *exits.*

ZOYA: You need to consume everything for yourself don't you, you can't have a minute where you're not swallowing everything in your path that you see.

RUBEN: As my Sponsor she has been very supportive.

ZOYA: To your penis muscle?

RUBEN: Why didn't you call me back once in a fucking lifetime?

None of this would have happened.

ZOYA: But it *did* happen, didn't it?

Because you can't stand a minute without being *adored!*

RUBEN: If you knew that then why'd you fucking leave me on my own?!

ZOYA: Because I wanted you to see what it is like! To be in this house, with you and your bottles, and feel completely *alone.* Ha! Man. You just wave suicide round like it's one of your ads, you think it gives you edge don't you? You're a fraud Ruben—it's so clear to me now.

VIRGINIA *enters. In Zoya's t-shirt and underpants.*

RUBEN: Jesus, Paul and Mary.

ZOYA: Yes, Ruben? What were you about to say?

Ok, then I will say something

VIRGINIA: Just say, 'I feel'.

ZOYA: What?

VIRGINIA: Start with 'I feel'.

Zoya.

We welcome your thoughts and feelings towards this situation. So—start with 'I feel'.

ZOYA: I feel like I'll start with whatever I want to start with speaking.

VIRGINIA: The 'I feel' language helps to establish an ease and neutrality to the communication.

ZOYA: 'I feel' I would like to know why are you wearing my t-shirt and knickers Virginia?

VIRGINIA: Are these yours?? I'm sorry, I'll take them off.

VIRGINIA *takes them off.*

ZOYA: Please! Keep them.

I will never be wearing them again anyway now.

VIRGINIA *stops.*

ZOYA: Scented candles.

VIRGINIA: Thank you.

ZOYA: Yeah, it's very, how to say.

Tranquil in here now.

You're fucking *my* fiancé in *my* bed, you know that?

RUBEN: Oh lord.

ZOYA: Or is that part of the *Program*?

As his Sponsor is that a very important stage of 'Growths'?

VIRGINIA: Ruben and I are deeply connected both inside and outside of the movement.

Ruben was open enough to tell me that he'd never actually connected sexually like this with anyone /prior to me, and I think that this previous lack of intimacy is a large contributor to his substance abuse trigger.

RUBEN: /Oh man.

ZOYA: Is this the truth?

VIRGINIA: We're looking into it at Group. If you ever want to join us, we'd

ZOYA: I will have my shirt back actually.

ZOYA *suddenly goes over to rip Virginia's t-shirt off—*

VIRGINIA: Don't you fucking touch me!

Slowly, VIRGINIA *takes the shirt off. Gives it to* ZOYA.

You can take the shirt. But you cannot take my husband.

ZOYA *looks to* RUBEN.

RUBEN: This is not a moment in my life where I feel *proud.*

Just to put that out there.

ZOYA: You two.

ZOYA *goes.*

VIRGINIA: You described her *so* well.

She really is *young.*

She seemed sweet enough though, in that *tall, skinny, model* way.

RUBEN: I don't think I'm one of you Virginia—I never have.

I think it's good that I don't drink now and I've really loved the talking, but I'm not like you guys—I can actually do things like write my book and go to work; I don't need to design my life around not shooting horse into my eyeball.

I was just going through a bad time and got carried away it's not pathological for me.

VIRGINIA: 'All Alcoholics use traumatic experiences to deem themselves powerless to Alcohol.'

RUBEN: What?

VIRGINIA: You're using Zoya and me to validate your desire to start drinking again.

I'm not going to let you Enable from this.

Not you.

Not Ruben Guthrie.

RUBEN *looks at her for a long time.*

RUBEN: You're good you are.

Just keep saving my life.

VIRGINIA: Your life is my life now.

END OF ACT THREE

ACT FOUR

4.1: MUM'S HOUSE

RUBEN: *Isolation…*
Isolation…
Men…
Isolation…
Bottle.
Isolation…
Message in a bottle.
Isolation…
Culture… Confusion… The pressure… The cunts… My mood…
Isolation…
Bottle the Isolation…
Bottle of Isolation?
Talk men.
Isolation…
Isolation /…
Sell…

MUM: /Beautiful words.
You could listen to it all day.

RUBEN: Why don't I read on a bit?
Drink. /Isol…

MUM: /No, that will do.

RUBEN: But you said.

MUM: I'm savouring.

RUBEN: It's been incredible to write it Mum, like it's pouring out of me,
I feel like I'm truly —

MUM: When are you going back to your Advertising job?

RUBEN: Mum, I'm a Poet now — it's real!

MUM: Making money is also real though Ruben, which is why I think
return to Subliminal and write your little poems on the side.

RUBEN: 'Little poems'!?
Mum, it's a work of poetic fiction! A novel in verse!

MUM: Oh darling, you should go to bed with a mirror and wake up to
yourself.

Ok. Clare Valley riesling.

Ruben?

Answer when someone speaks to you.

RUBEN: What?

MUM: Yes or no?

RUBEN: Mum, what the fuck are you—

MUM: Just a little glass with your mum.

RUBEN: Huh?

MUM: Huh?

RUBEN: *You* were the one that took me to my first meeting!

And now you're Enabling me, why are you Enabling me?

MUM: Ruben, sit down.

I said sit down here.

> RUBEN *sits down near* MUM. *She pours a glass of wine for him, puts it before him.*

This is a glass of wine. /That's all it is.

That girl you're with may call it something else but I call it a glass of wine.

RUBEN: /Ohh!

Her name is Virginia Mum.

MUM: I don't like her.

And I don't like who you're turning into the more you spend time with her.

You drank a little too much at a certain point in your life so you put yourself through a process and that was so brave. Now it is time for you to re-enter society and drink rationally.

RUBEN: But Mum I can't drink /rationally.

MUM: /I'm your mother and I love you.

RUBEN: I love you too Mum.

MUM: But these meetings, they fill your head with so much hogwash; you come home blaming your parents for all sorts of things.

RUBEN: Mum, if I have a glass of wine, it will all start again!

MUM: No, it won't.

RUBEN: How won't it?

MUM: Don't let it!

Just don't *let it.*

RUBEN: Mum, you need to face it. I'm an—

MUM: No.

RUBEN: Mum

MUM: No you are not.

RUBEN: I'm an…

MUM: Uht!

>No son of mine is one of them.

>Not in my lifetime.

>Now!

>MUM *holds out a glass of wine for him.*

RUBEN: Mum, don't do this to me—I'm in such good shape.
  /I like my life I like myself.

MUM: /Your father and I have decided enough of those meetings.
>We'd like our son back now.

RUBEN: Since when did you and Dad start talking again?

MUM: Since he… since Peter moved back in.

RUBEN: What?

MUM: Well SHE wasn't going to look after him, was she?

RUBEN: Mum…

MUM: He's a sick man!

RUBEN: You got that right!
>/Fucking—

MUM: /Don't think you understand everything Ruben because you don't.
>There are things in a marriage that /you don't see…

RUBEN: /Pathetic…

MUM: He's my husband!

RUBEN: He left you!

MUM: Well, why wouldn't he?
>I'm old—I look old—I sound old.
>And I don't feel so sexual your father likes sex.

RUBEN: Mum!

MUM: Age has spikes Ruben.
>Now come and have a little glass of wine and then a glass of
  water.

RUBEN: I can't believe this.

MUM: Glass of wine glass of water then bed.

RUBEN: Your father drank himself into oblivion and then Dad!
>Remember the nights?

MUM: You're not them Son.
>You're different.
>You're Ruben Guthrie.
RUBEN: Ruben Guthrie. Just feels. Too big. For his skin. Can't. Fit.
MUM: Women don't like poetry Ruben.
>We like *story*.
>Character.
>Driven.
>Story.

> MUM *pours wine into her son's mouth.* RUBEN *lets her. It rolls about in his mouth.*

> MUM *kisses him and leaves.*

> *Pause.*

> RUBEN *spits out the wine!*

4.2: ZOYA'S APARTMENT IN PRAGUE

RUBEN *climbs in the window. Clunk. Snow.*

ZOYA: Hello Klauss? Just finishing my make-up!

> ZOYA *enters dressed up.*

>Holy moly! Ruben?
RUBEN: No, I'm an apparition.
ZOYA: How did you get into the apartment?
RUBEN: Window.
>Your apartment is high up!
>Terrifying climb in the snow.
ZOYA: You're my hero.
RUBEN: Just give me ten minutes.
ZOYA: Leave now!
RUBEN: Five minutes.
ZOYA: No minutes.
RUBEN: Two minutes.
ZOYA: One minute.
RUBEN: You look incredible.
ZOYA: I don't give so much of a fuck.
RUBEN: Where are you off to?

ZOYA: Screening of a documentary film about child soldiers.

At my college.

And then we will have a party.

RUBEN: To celebrate the child soldiers?

ZOYA: Why would we celebrate child soldiers?

RUBEN: No matter—can I come with you?

ZOYA: I can't believe you're in Prague.

RUBEN: I can't believe I left it this long.

ZOYA: Well you were busy with your Sponsor.

RUBEN: We broke up—she moved out.

ZOYA: Ohhh, why?

RUBEN: Because my heart.

Pause.

ZOYA: That's a big *shame* it didn't work out between you and the fugly crackhead.

Sounds like you guys had a really 'connected' time together.

RUBEN: Zoya, think back.

ZOYA: To the time of the Aztecs? What period in history are we…

RUBEN: I don't expect you to come running

But I just wanted to let you know.

There is no other you in this world.

ZOYA *laughs.*

What?

ZOYA: Show some ironies or some kind of subtext if you're going to make it as writer. 'There is no other you.' No shit!

Pause.

RUBEN: So you're a big grown-up documentary girl now?

ZOYA: Soon I will be a documentary maker, yes.

RUBEN: Documentary is interesting.

ZOYA: What the fuck do you know about documentary? All you watch is cartoons.

RUBEN: I've seen plenty of foreign docos   /I watch foreign.

ZOYA: /Ha! Which foreign?

RUBEN: Well I can't pronounce them all because they're so foreign.

ZOYA: Yeah right.

RUBEN: *March of the Penguins.*

ZOYA: That's not foreign!

RUBEN: They're in the Arctic!

ZOYA: My lecturer loves that film.

RUBEN: Who is your lecturer? //Older guy or—

ZOYA: //It's so prophetic.

  So poetic that film, I…

RUBEN: I watched it on the plane here!

ZOYA: Good!

RUBEN: It's about these penguins and this march that they do—see for some unknown and really deep reason these penguins choose to live in an endless, hellish blizzard.

ZOYA: Ruben, I know I've seen it.

RUBEN: You've seen it?

ZOYA: Everyone has seen it.

RUBEN: How fucking great is it?

ZOYA: It's ok.

RUBEN: I cried!

ZOYA: Structurally, it's very American.

RUBEN: How's that fucking bit where the female penguin FINALLY comes home!

ZOYA: Yes. And—

RUBEN: And all the men penguins they are squeaking like crazy—and he's been holding the little baby penguin egg between his feet for like forever.

ZOYA: And they're all packed together like a wall of penguin.

RUBEN: But she knows exactly which penguin is hers just from listening.

ZOYA: To the sound of him.

RUBEN: To the sound of him.

  Penguin noises.

ZOYA: And then the egg cracks open—crack!

RUBEN: And the little baby penguin comes out.

ZOYA: And the mother vomits fish up for her little baby—and the baby feeds on the mother's vomit—oh and then there is this divine moment!

RUBEN: Yes!

ZOYA: Where the parent penguins…

RUBEN: They stand together!

ZOYA: For like a minute!
RUBEN: With the baby penguin between them.
   Long pause.
RUBEN: And then…
ZOYA: I don't love you anymore.
RUBEN: And then the ahh…what happens?
ZOYA: I'm going to be late for my film.
RUBEN: Yes! He waddles off to the lake.
ZOYA: Who does?
RUBEN: He's been waiting.
ZOYA: Ruben, I must —
RUBEN: In the blizzard for so long.

    Pause.

ZOYA: He must be hungry then.
RUBEN: He is hungry.
    So fucking hungry.
    And thirsty.

4.3: A KITCHEN

Empty stage for a time.

Finally, RUBEN *enters.*

RUBEN *takes an icy-cold beer out of an icy-cold fridge. It's so fucking cold. Steam rises off it.*

RUBEN *takes the beer in his hand and looks at it. Cold and beautiful.*

RUBEN *screws the lid off the beer. The noise it makes.*

Time stops.

RUBEN *drinks the beer. Savouring every bit of it. Time passes as he drinks the beer.*

RUBEN *exclaims massive sighs of relief and passion.*

Finally, when the beer is done, RUBEN *sings.*

RUBEN: *Put on my blue suede shoes and I boarded the plane… Touched down in the land of the Delta Blues in the middle of the pouring rain. W.C. Handy won't let you look down over me. Yeah I got a first-class ticket but I'm as blue as a boy can be.*

Then I'm walking in Memphis, *Was walking with my feet ten feet off of Beale, Walking in Memphis… But do I really feel the way I feel?*

DAMIAN *enters carrying a table packed with various drugs (miles of coke and meth and pills). He sets the table down, singing.*

DAMIAN: *Saw the ghost of Elvis on Union Avenue… Followed him up to the gates of the Graceland then I watched him walk right through. Now security they did not see him… they just hovered round his tomb… but there's a pretty little thing… waiting for The King… down in the Jungle Room!*

RUBEN *and* DAMIAN *unite for the second chorus.*

DAMIAN & RUBEN: *Then I'm walking in Memphis… Was walking with my feet ten feet off of Beale, Walking in Memphis… But do I really feel the way I feel?*

RUBEN *has two or three bottles in his hands at any one time. He drinks from various bottles constantly. This has been going on for weeks. Months even.*

DAMIAN: We have the ability to change everything, you and I, because we have all the *ideas!*

You know how hard it is for some people to have an *idea?*

RUBEN: I have no *idea.*

DAMIAN: LAUGH OUT LOUD!

RUBEN & DAMIAN: Hahahahahahahahahahahahahahahahahhahahaha!

RUBEN: I love you man.

DAMIAN: Ohh baby, don't go doing the coke love /speech, baby?

RUBEN: /I always loved you.

And I'm sorry I got lost with the whole 'Virginia loves the Lord' thing!

DAMIAN: I knew you'd come back baby, you're my boy.

RUBEN: I. No—hear me out!

I love you, so deep inside my heart.

And I think it's important you and I continue to get smashed.

SMASHED: *Out of our tiny skulls.*

Smash the world into pieces so we can *see,* through the cracks, into the light of *ideas.*

DAMIAN: We can only do that by getting smashed.

RUBEN: Smashing it up so we can *see* into it!

DAMIAN: We can do *anything* Ruben; you realise that?

RUBEN: I know.

> Come here.

> DAMIAN *crawls over to him on all fours.* RUBEN *holds his face close.*

It's weird isn't it?

> The more you know someone, the more you love and adore them.

DAMIAN: Yeah baby.

RUBEN: The more you love and adore them, the more you want to hurt them.

> /Really badly.

DAMIAN: /I adore your eyes.

> So intense, like you can see into us.

> *Us* wanton fools.

> DAMIAN *starts kissing* RUBEN. RUBEN *kisses back then pushes him off.*

RUBEN: Don't fag out on me man—how many times.

DAMIAN: Remember the Tourism ad we made baby?

> *'You'll never never know, if you never never go'.*

RUBEN: We need more 'caine!

DAMIAN: There's still three grams on the table!

> /And all the METH!

RUBEN: /Fucking need so much more—call every dealer you know ask for everything they have!

> RUBEN *rips open a huge back of meth and smears it all over his face, inhaling.*

Out of our tiny skulls!

DAMIAN: Man, you're losing all the meth on your face and the floor!

RUBEN: So get more!

> Where cigarettes?

DAMIAN: Just here. Where?

> I got ten cartons when was that day I got the ten cartons?

RUBEN: It was raining.

DAMIAN: I'll go up the B.P. Shell. The Caltex. The B.P.! Haha!

> Wait here!

> DAMIAN *kisses* RUBEN.

RUBEN: Hey!

DAMIAN: Yeah.

RUBEN: We gotta get the band back together!

DAMIAN: YES!!!!!! OH MY GOD WE FUCKEN' DO!

RUBEN & DAMIAN: *Papa Don't Preach—the '80s experience!*

> DAMIAN *exits.* RUBEN *unscrews the lid off a bottle of vodka and drinks hard from it.*

RUBEN: I don't give a fuck I fucken.
> Get a good job boyo.
> Put your money away in your special SAVER account SAVER.
> Find a girl a girl a girl.
> Tick the boxes tick the boxes.
> Have a kid have a kid just the one!
> Call it something unusual, unusual, unusual.
> Wheel it down the beach the beach the beach.
> Be good to your parents your parents.
> The Mummy and the Daddy Daddy Daddy.
> Sing the silent roar keep it all inside.
> Till the day you die die die.

> RUBEN *drinks from the vodka.*

I am the future.
> I am the fucked-up future.
> And nothing can touch me.

VIRGINIA: True.

> RUBEN *sings the first verse and chorus of 'Eternal Flame' to her.*

I just came to pick up my turn tables.
> I think that's the last of my stuff.
> This is your last chance Ruben.
> Or burn here.

MUM: //Darling it's me.
> ///Darling I need you to let me in the apartment.

ZOYA: Hello Ruben? It is me calling.

RUBEN: Hombre!

ZOYA: I am so sad when Susan tells me this.

MUM: I don't blame you Ruben.

RUBEN: *I don't blame you!*

ZOYA: Don't blame me Ruben.

MUM: Your father is very worried about you also.

RUBEN: Where fuck is cunt?

ZOYA: I never said go.

RUBEN: Face up.

ZOYA: This some elaborate cry for help? Because if it is—

PETER: Answer the phone next time I call you.

      You think I have hours in my day to leave /voicemails.

RUBEN: /Red wine? White wine? G & T?

VIRGINIA: Ken started using again.

      Lost hope he said.

PETER: Your mother's worried about you.

MUM: Please let your mother in, it's cold out here darling?

VIRGINIA: Janelle thinks she failed you.

PETER: The whole restaurant is worried about you.

RAY: Ruben Guthrie it's me!

      Hey, I saw my boy.

RUBEN: Awwwwwww!

RAY: I called her up!

      And she said 'alright you can see him'.

VIRGINIA: It's ok Ruben.

MUM: Hello you.

VIRGINIA: We all hide away when we relapse.

      We feel ashamed so we hide out.

ZOYA: Will you call me please?

RAY: He wants to meet you.

ZOYA: Even if you're angry and you want to scream at a girl.

      RUBEN *screams at her.*

RAY: No good being in here Son.

RUBEN: Offer you a drink Ray?

ZOYA: There is a snowstorm tonight.

VIRGINIA: Pellegrino waits for you!

MUM: Open a window at least?

VIRGINIA: At the door with his /ears up.

ZOYA: /A blizzard.

RUBEN: Step away from the fucking windows!

MUM: Ok!

RAY: I was a monster on the sauce.

ZOYA: Is this *March of the Penguins*?

PETER: But I tell you one thing I don't sit at home drinking all day and feeling sorry for myself!

VIRGINIA: Everything I touch.

RAY: You want me to tell you what I did to her face?

ZOYA: I can hear you.

PETER: I get on with it!

MUM: Lift up!

VIRGINIA: Everything I love.

RUBEN: Get off me you fuck!

ZOYA: Come find me in the snow.

RAY: Buckley? Hendrix?

ZOYA: I'll have a puffy jacket on.

VIRGINIA: Everybody /leaves!

RUBEN: /Isolation! Isolation! Isolation! Iso—

MUM *pours a bucket of water over him.*

Weak as piss!

PETER: I'm sorry I sent you away!

RUBEN: I'm coming up Corey.

PETER: Ruben Guthrie?

RUBEN: See you soon Corey.

PETER: I just wanted the best.

RUBEN: Chill out Corey!

DAMIAN *enters with eight cartons of cigarettes on his shoulder.*

DAMIAN: Who's Corey? Corey Hart?

DAMIAN *sings the opening of 'Sunglasses at Night' and* RUBEN *shovels coke and ice into his head.*

Baby, baby chill.

RUBEN: *'See your doctor if pain persists.'*

DAMIAN *grabs* RUBEN, *pulls him away from the drugs.*

DAMIAN: Ruben, baby—it's me!

RUBEN: *'You can get it milking a cow, matter of fact—I got it now.'*

DAMIAN *pulls* RUBEN *onto the couch.*

DAMIAN: Shhhhh…

RUBEN: What're those yellow pills on the table?

DAMIAN: Sleeping tablets for elephants and horses.

/We'll take a half tomorrow.

RUBEN: /I'm not sleeping.

Hear that? Ruben Guthrie is not sleeping!

DAMIAN: Dust down baby dust down.

In the mouth of the quiet.

They sit in the mouth of the quiet.

I'm going to admit something.

About New York.

I lied to you, about…

RUBEN: The Instant Messenger thing.

Yeah, I know.

DAMIAN: How do you know that?

RUBEN: I see people.

I see into their heads.

To the hiding.

DAMIAN: Can't we just try some kissing?

RUBEN: Go and stand over by the bench.

DAMIAN: You stand by the bench.

RUBEN: Now BITCH!

DAMIAN *gets up, and goes over to the bench.*

DAMIAN: Ok. I'm 'by the bench'!

RUBEN: Bend over the bench.

DAMIAN: Are you *toying* with me baby?

RUBEN: Pull your pants down.

If you want this to happen, you've got a window.

RUBEN *picks up the bag of yellow sleeping pills.*

DAMIAN: Baby, this is going to clear all the confusion for you.

RUBEN: Right down— both.

RUBEN *starts swallowing the yellow sleeping pills.*

DAMIAN: I can't wait to feel this.

RUBEN: Bend right out.

DAMIAN: You've done this before?

RUBEN *takes more pills. Washing them down with vodka.*

RUBEN: That's nice, I *like* that baby.

DAMIAN: I can feel you getting closer!

RUBEN: I'm so close Corey.

> DAMIAN *turns around.* RUBEN *has collapsed.*

DAMIAN: Ruben Guthrie!

END OF ACT FOUR

ACT FIVE

5.1: A church hall/visitors' area.

MUM: Hello my name is Susan and I am the wife of an Alcoholic and the daughter of an Alcoholic—I must have a type!

Sometimes I think it's me, sometimes I think yes they can drink normally, sometimes I get so mad I try to convince myself that I don't care at all.

Fooling myself. As a parent I wanted to protect my child but it was not possible.

Of course it was him as well how could it not be!

I am very grateful to be here. I really I am.

It's nice to talk to others living in this nightmare.

Because it *is* a nightmare.

When you are a mother and you love your son with all your heart and you are sitting in a cold, grey, antiseptic hospital waiting room with a cup of brown, flavourless coffee in your hand and your son's body moves past you on a tray. A tray on wheels his flesh his little hands his face… moving… past… and you think…

Where did I go wrong?

Where along the line did I lose my grip?

PETER: Coming through!

> PETER *wheels his drip in to the hospital visitors' area.*

Ey?

MUM: Have a seat.

PETER: Can hardly sit anywhere, the tubes…

> MUM *watches* PETER*'s legs slip in and out of the gown.*

MUM: You've got quite nice legs Peter.

PETER: Alright.

MUM: You should get around in a patient's smock more often.

PETER: You enjoying this?

> PETER *sits, with difficulty.*

MUM: Oh, you're a wimp!

PETER: You try having tubes from the back of your nose to your abdomen!

MUM: Our son.

PETER: Yep.

MUM: God I hate Alcohol. I hate it.

> *Long pause.*

> PETER *starts to cry.* MUM *doesn't comfort him. She just faces out. Eventually,* PETER *stops crying.*

PETER: Did the mud crab come in from De Costi's?

> MUM *nods.*

The abalone?

> MUM *nods.*

The blue-eyed cod?

MUM: All of it!

PETER: Good!

> *Finally,* RUBEN *enters, with difficulty, on a drip.*

MUM: Here, let me…

RUBEN: I'm right.

> RUBEN *sits. Long pause.*

MUM: What did the doctor say?

PETER: You're a fucken idiot?

> RUBEN *just looks at his dad. Pause.*

MUM: Overdose?

RUBEN: Said I overdosed on the sleeping pills yeah.
And that…That if I drink again I might die.

PETER: Pffft! They said that to me too, and I'm alright.

MUM: You just had a major operation.
You nearly died!

PETER: Settle down, people are sleeping in the wards.

> MUM *slaps* PETER *across the head.*

MUM: Don't you fucking order me around again!
PETER: Fuck.

Pause.

MUM: I'm going to talk to the doctors.
See if I can get some brochures.

MUM *kisses* RUBEN *on the head and goes.*

Long silence.

PETER: Have a hit of this bad boy!

PETER *unveils a small bottle of spirits.*

RUBEN: Peter!
PETER: Don't make a racket.
RUBEN: What have you got a flask of that for?
PETER: Because they don't serve wines by the glass in this joint.
RUBEN: Peter, look where we are!
PETER: So be quick.
RUBEN: Dad.
PETER: Think of it like one of those ads you make.
You know the ones!
About how people do extreme things to get what they truly desire.
RUBEN: Dad, I can't... what is it?

PETER *takes a nip then places the flask on the chair next to* RUBEN.

PETER: I better go find your mother.

PETER *goes to go.*

RUBEN: Dad.
PETER: Yep?
RUBEN: Why are you doing this?
PETER: Doing what?

RUBEN *refers to the flask.*

I don't know Son.
I don't know anything else.

PETER *goes.*

Long pause.

RUBEN *bats the flask off the chair, sending it onto the floor.*

Long pause.

RUBEN *sits and looks at the flask.*

Long pause.

RUBEN *stretches out his body, finally clasping the flask between his feet and dragging it slowly back towards the chair.*

RUBEN *props the flask up with his feet.*

RUBEN *picks up the flask.*

RUBEN *unscrews the lid and sniffs the contents.*

RUBEN *goes to drink.* RUBEN *does not drink and pushes the flask down with great difficulty.*

RUBEN *holds the flask.*

Long pause.

RUBEN *looks up and speaks softly to the audience.*

RUBEN: My name is Ruben Guthrie and I am....

Fade to black.

THE END